"A HAPPY THOUGHT"
THE STORY OF THE BARKING HISTORICAL SOCIETY
1934 - 1994

by

Herbert Hope Lockwood

Front Cover Illustration: Roding Lodge, North Street - home of the Hewett family from around 1870 to 1957. Coloured sketch from Frogley MS.

Rear Cover Illustration: Paul Tully (Hon. Treasurer 1967-1991), Dorothy and Herbert Lockwood with B. & D.H.S. display at Essex History Fair, Maldon, 1991.

Published by the author from:

10 Alloa Road, Goodmayes, Ilford, Essex IG3 9SP

FOREWORD

It is a particular pleasure to commend this publication. The extensive research undertaken by our Vice-President H.H. (Bert) Lockwood has enabled him to describe not only the story of this Society in detail over the last 60 years but something of the progress of exploration of Barking's past which will be of great use and interest to us now and for generations to come.

G.S. Sanders-Hewett
President
Barking & District Historical Society

AUTHOR'S PREFACE

The opinions expressed in this book are my own and do not necessarily represent the views of the Officers or the Committee of the Barking and District Historical Society.

H.H. Lockwood
Vice-President

(C) Herbert Hope Lockwood 1994

ISBN 0 9516483 1 4

GENESIS

The BARKING AND DISTRICT ARCHAEOLOGICAL SOCIETY was founded sixty years ago by the coming together of a somewhat diverse group of local history enthusiasts. None of them were archaeologists in the now commonly accepted sense - hence the change of name in more recent times to BARKING HISTORICAL SOCIETY (and then to BARKING AND DISTRICT HISTORICAL SOCIETY). But the original name was doubtless borrowed from the old established Essex Archaeological Society of which several were already members.

It is no accident that the birth of the B. & D.A.S. in 1934 followed closely upon the achievement of Borough status by the town in 1931. It could be expected that such a civic occasion should be accompanied by public celebrations in a mood of communal self-congratulation and pride in past history. In the Barking of 1931 these took the form - besides the customary processions, illuminations and fireworks - of an Historical Pageant and an Industrial Exhibition. The Pageant - Eleven Scenes and an Epilogue - was presented nightly in Barking Park for a whole week and hundreds of citizens and their children were actors in this spectacular production.

Most of the future founders of the Barking Archaeological were deeply involved in these celebrations as organisers or participants. Most chiefly concerned in civic organisation by virtue of his office was the Charter Town Clerk, Stephen Jewers. Part of the official preparations was the publication of a souvenir Book of Barking to commemorate the occasion and introduce the Pageant, and he himself wrote the first chapter summarising the history of local government in Barking up to the Borough Charter. He obviously found this history congenial and continued research into the records - a few years later the new Borough Council published another souvenir book by him entitled, A Century of Progress in Local Government in Barking 1835-1935, commemorating the Municipal Corporations Act of 1835. By the time it appeared Jewers had already become the first Hon. Treasurer of the new Archaeological Society of which, as we shall see, he was a prime mover - he occupied the Chair 1937-38, and took over as Hon. Secretary in 1939.

The second chapter of the Book of Barking, 'Some Notes on the History of Barking', was written by the doyen of local historians, Fred Brand. Born in 1857, the son of a North Street grocer, a Church organist in Loughton for over 30 years, and finally resident in Ilford, he had joined the Essex Archaeological Society back in 1899. A modest and kindly man with many self-taught skills, he had busied himself collecting Essex books and manuscripts, and compiling his 4-

volume Essex Index, copies of which were duplicated and bound by himself and which, until 1959, was the best county bibliography in existence. He also wrote and printed booklets on historical subjects, took photographs and painted. He was an obvious choice for membership of the Historical Committee of the Barking Pageant.

James OXLEY with Fred BRAND in Brand's study in Ilford c.1934

The following year - 1932 - Brand became Chairman of a further Historical Committee when Barking teamed up with her neighbours, Ilford and Dagenham (where the village had expanded into the huge L.C.C. Becontree Estate), to run the Pageant of Essex in aid of the new King George V Hospital. For this he wrote the introduction, 'This Essex of Ours', and the story of Episode 1 - 'Boadicea' (which the writer can still recollect seeing as a child in Valentines Park, Ilford). Serving with Brand were Dorothy M. Hobbs, who had written the words of Ilford's Charter Day Song, 'In Unity Progress', in 1926, and Capt. A. W. Amies, the L.C.C.'s Resident Agent in Becontree. These three were also to become founder members of the Barking and District Archaeological Society. Fred Brand then served successively as Vice-Chairman and Chairman of the new society and was uniquely honoured by a Vice-Presidency and Life Membership not long before his death in 1939.

The chapter on 'Barking Abbey' in the Book of Barking was written by the acknowledged expert on this subject, Col. E. A. Loftus, the dynamic headmaster of Barking Abbey School whose interest in the Abbey seems to have been particularly motivated by the naming of his school in 1922. Loftus wrote the story and most of the dialogue for eight of the eleven scenes in the Barking Pageant since these dealt mainly with the history of the Abbey. Scene 4 was in fact enacted largely by staff and pupils of his school - the boys no doubt enjoyed rushing on as Danish raiders even more than the girls enjoyed fleeing as weeping nuns. For the Pageant of Essex he wrote the yet more spectacular Episode 4, 'Queen Elizabeth at Tilbury'. Not surprisingly, Ernest Loftus was also a founder of the B. & D.A.S., served on its first committee, and was eventually to be elected its third President in 1953.

This elevation followed the death of Robert Muirhead Hewett, the head of the family who had built up the Short Blue Fleet which had once made Barking the greatest fishing port in Britain. But Robert Hewett was also a more than capable historian of the industry. His contribution to the Book of Barking in 1931 on 'Barking as a Fishing Port' is as good a short history as anything ever written on the subject. He was to become the first Chairman of the Society and later succeeded Lord Salisbury as its second President. His son, Douglas Hewett, was an active member, and our President today, Mr G. S. Sanders-Hewett, known to his many friends as 'Pip', is a grandson.

The Book of Barking also contained a chapter on 'Barking Charities' written by Alexander Glenny. He was Clerk to the Barking Charities - as his father, Samuel, had been before him and as his son, Kenneth, was to be after him (his grandson Keith is the present Clerk!). It is probable that Alexander was a founder member of the B. & D.A.S. but he died early in 1935 and our earliest complete membership list dates from 1938/39. However by that time his son, Kenneth, was a member and destined to become President of the Society from 1958 until his death in 1977 - more will be said about him later in this history.

The other branch of the Glenny family was represented by George W. Glenny who was Vice-Chairman of King George V Hospital. He was the son of the Barking market gardener and Essex County Alderman, William Wallis Glenny (1839-1923), an enthusiastic local historian who had contributed frequently to the Essex Review and written the sections on 'Market Gardening' and 'Sea Fisheries' (not by a Hewett!) for Vol.2 of the Victoria County History of Essex in 1907. He would have no doubt been delighted by the inauguration of the B. & D.H.S. in 1934 had he lived to see it.

Robert Muirhead HEWETT J.P. Chairman 1934-35. President 19??-1952.

There were however several men important in the early story of the Society who played no part in the Charter celebrations. One of them was a young Yorkshireman with an M.A. from Sheffield called James Oxley - later Dr James Oxley - who arrived in Barking between 1931 and 1934 to take up a post at Gascoigne School. Teaching History there and seeking local examples he soon became interested in Barking history and made the acquaintance of local enthusiasts. He received much encouragement from Brand and Jewers, less from Loftus. The elderly Fred Brand in particular welcomed the expert assistance of a keen young man with the academic training that he himself lacked. On similar grounds Loftus scented a potential rival. But James Oxley was elected the first Secretary of the Archaeological Society and the Editor of its Transactions and more will be said later about the importance of his contribution. Sad to relate he passed away in June 1994.

This means, incidentally, that the only surviving original member is now Mr C. H. Chown who was elected to the Committee in 1939 when he was living at Chigwell. Though still a young man when the Barking Society was formed he had already established himself as an authority on the Lethieullier family with articles in the Essex Review in 1926 and 1927. He is, I am delighted to observe, still very much alive and we hope to see him during the anniversary celebrations.

Mr Claude H.I. CHOWN, founder member, as a young man in 1937. Member 1934-1994. Vice-President.

"A HAPPY THOUGHT"

It might appear from what has already been said that by 1934 the formation of the Barking and District Archaeological Society was an event waiting to happen. The catalyst was a visit to Barking on 6 October by the British Archaeological Society for which arrangements had been made by Jewers as Town Clerk.

Stephen A. JEWERS, (Barking Town Clerk 1929-1940). Hon.Treasurer 1934-35. Chairman 1937-38. Hon.Secretary 1938-39.

Many of the local people mentioned previously had been invited to the reception. Colonel Loftus conducted the party around the Abbey site, although "rain was falling heavily at the time". After tea Robert Hewett rebuked the Mayor for an ill-timed attempt to defend the demolition of the Elizabethan Court House (then usually referred to as the Old Town Hall) in the course of his official speech of welcome. This, though it had taken place back in 1923, still rankled with some older inhabitants. More constructively, the Town Clerk seized the occasion to initiate amongst the local residents present "a discussion as to the desirability of forming a society, or group, farther to explore the historical records of the district". Having secured initial interest he undertook to summons a meeting if he got sufficient support. In a naive but memorable sentence the Barking Advertiser reflected, "It will be remembered that the origin of the Society arose from a happy thought by the Town Clerk".

So on the 10th November the inaugural meeting took place with Robert Hewett in the Chair. The Constitution of the society subsequently adopted declared that, "The objects of the Society shall be the study of archaeology, more particularly of Barking and district (viz., Beacontree Hundred) and other places known to be associated with old Barking". There is no doubt that they were using the word 'archaeology' in its older and wider sense of the study of history through the use of records as well as excavation. In modern terms they appear in effect to be defining themselves as a Local Historical and Archaeological Society. But it is equally evident that the enthusiastic core were mainly interested in further exploring the history of Barking from primary documentary sources.

PRIME

A great deal was achieved during the first five years of the Society's existence. There were 47 members during the initial year and there was a modest increase to 57 by 1938/9 - obviously there had been no drive towards mass membership. The list for 1938/39 reveals a number of 'official' members: the Town Clerk, Borough Education Officer and Borough Engineer of Barking; the Town Clerk of Ilford; the Clerk to the Council of Dagenham; five Librarians; and an assortment of teachers and clergy. Nevertheless many of these were active members and overall the ratio of 'active' to 'passive' membership seems to have been high.

The inclusion of 'and District' in the title and the reference to 'Beacontree Hundred' in the Objects were not just wishful thinking. Almost 60% of the members in 1938/9 came from outside the Borough of Barking; over a quarter came from Ilford. This is partly to be explained by the absence at that time of any similar society nearer than the Walthamstow Antiquarian Society (established 1914). But doubtless many Ilfordians were aware that most of the earlier history of Barking was equally their history. It is certainly true that 'outsiders' have played a significant part in the Society throughout its history and continue to do so despite the more recent formation of other local history societies within the ancient bounds of Becontree Hundred.

Lord Salisbury, a major landowner in Barking, consented to become first President, and the initial list of Vice-Presidents included 4 Bishops, the Lord of the Manor (Sir. H. Westrow-Hulse), and a former M.P. Official encouragement from the Borough of Barking extended to allowing the Society to use the Council Chamber for meetings.

The usual pattern of monthly meetings with lectures (often illustrated) and excursions was quickly established. Three of the seven lectures during the first year were delivered by members: Brand spoke on 'Parish Church Architecture', Loftus on 'Barking Abbey', and Oxley on 'Some Barking Documents'. Oxley had taken on the task of Editor as well as Secretary and this lecture showed that he had already acquired a formidable grasp of Barking documentation in the medieval period at least. Most of the photographs of records with which he illustrated his lecture were specially taken for him by Brand.

According to the Barking Advertiser which was giving excellent coverage to Society meetings at the time, "the lecturer said that an investigation of the printed histories of the town showed that little had been added since the early Eighteenth Century, and a great deal which passed for history had no basis at all in documentary evidence". Towards the end of the lecture he spoke of, "the slack way in which the history of the Abbey had been written, showing clearly how much remained for the Society to do".

The very next year, Oxley produced a short History of Barking based mainly on his own reading and research into records, although he is generous in his acknowledgements to Brand and Jewers. Whilst describing it as "only a pamphlet", a reviewer in the The Times said, "In forty-six small pages Mr Oxley has packed an astonishing amount of Barking's history". And in the Transactions for 1936 and 1937 he continued to set the pace by publishing his transcript of the 'Barking Abbey Rental of 1456' which Brand had purchased at auction in 1923 but of which only a few extracts had hitherto been printed. The transcript itself represented a major task and occupied more than 60 pages of print but Oxley was right to regard the Rental as "one of the most important Barking documents extant". No other contains the names of so many inhabitants of medieval Barking and it is the earliest source for many minor place-names in Ilford and Barking. The present writer confesses that the challenge of locating some of the places named was one of the first things which attracted him into local history.

*(Dr) James E.
OXLEY M.A.
Hon.Secretary
1934-38.
Hon.Editor.
Vice-President
1952-1994*

In 1936 and 1938 lectures were delivered on Dagenham history by John O'Leary, another member of the Society with keen enthusiasm for exploring the records. A flamboyant character, first and only Chief Librarian of Dagenham, he seized the opportunity of the opening of a new Civic Centre in 1937 to get the Dagenham Council to publish his <u>Book of Dagenham</u> - a model local history in its day which eventually ran through three editions. He also persuaded the Council to open a Museum in Valence House since it was no longer required for Council Offices.

Barking had already opened a Museum at Eastbury House, on lease from the National Trust, in 1935. This was another project to which Jewers had given strong support, and the Curator, H. B. Johnson, became a member of the Committee of the B. & D.A.S.

SURVIVAL AND REVIVAL

But this brief "golden age" of local history was ended - like so many other things - by the outbreak of war in 1939. Younger members were called up, older members found themselves engaged in war service in some form or another, travel restrictions and black-out made excursions and meetings impracticable. With the cessation of the printed Transactions and Minutes which provide us with so much knowledge of the pre-war years our ignorance becomes almost complete. Even our information on the immediate post-war period is scrappy and incomplete. We presume the Society was in a state of suspension. The Eastbury House Museum was closed after its very brief life, its Curator transferred to library duties and the collection dispersed. But in Dagenham the Valence House museum survived.

For reasons not directly attributable to the War, Stephen Jewers resigned as Town Clerk and went into private practice whilst that grand old man, Fred Brand, died at the end of 1939. His fine library was ultimately bought by Ilford Libraries to become the nucleus of their Local History Collection. But he had given away certain gems of his collection: notably the 1456 Abbey Rent Roll to British Museum's Department of Manuscripts, and the Frogley MS to the Library of the Essex Archaeological Society. This latter seems to have been acquired by Brand in the '30s and, uncharacteristically, he was reticent about it even to his friend Oxley - perhaps he had intended to edit it and publish it himself.

Oxley went into the R.A.F. On completing his service he took a post as Lecturer in Westminster Training College and, although able to visit Barking only occasionally, he continued to act as Editor to the Society after the War.

A first glimmer of revival came in 1944 when the architect H. H. Dawson, a founder member and Chairman 1938/39, addressed a meeting on 'William Mead, Quaker, upholder of the rights of Juries'. It is possible that Jewers, still practising in Barking, was in the chair. Even then we have no direct evidence for several years that the Society was meeting regularly. When we have, we find that the Secretary was W. G. Fairchild who moved from Deputy to Chief Librarian of Barking in 1947. He had, it is interesting to note, entered the Barking Libraries as a Junior Assistant straight from Barking Abbey School in 1926. He ran the Society until 1965 although, curiously, he seems to have had no great enthusiasm for local history himself - it is said that he often quitted the meeting after making the announcements at the start. From c.1958 Miss Joan Harrison, then a new member, took and typed up the AGM minutes.

For a number of years Miss Harrison also performed the often unrewarding task of Publicity Officer. It is a pleasure to record that she is still an active member, cheerfully making the awkward journey from her Barkingside home to each meeting.

In 1948/9 we discover Robert Hewett still President and John G. O'Leary serving as Chairman. The programme that season included a lecture by the latter on 'Monastic Foundations in Essex', another by Doctor James Oxley on 'Life in Barking Abbey', and a talk by F. G. Emmison, the Essex County Archivist, on 'The Detailed Inventory of William Pownsett of Loxford, 1554'. Meetings were now held in the Magazine Room on the first floor of the Central Library (opened 1924) in Ripple Road.

The loyalty of original pre-war members who helped to 'keep the show on the road' after the War is worthy of remark. Cecil Hustwayte of Barkingside serving as Programme Secretary until his death in 1968 took a good deal off the shoulders of Secretary Fairchild. And the record for service must surely go to S. E. Lloyd of Goodmayes who, elected as Treasurer back in 1938, was still doing the job when he was seriously injured by a car in 1962. Mrs Hustwayte then took over this office until she died in 1967.

After 1952 John O'Leary became too busy with his other tasks to take the Chair, and handed over to his Vice-Chairman, Ernest Gowers. The latter was the Barking born manager to Kenneth Glenny the auctioneer and estate-agent, having started work with Ken's father, Alexander, back in 1905. He had been a Barking Councillor since 1938. In 1958 when he was granted the rare honour of being made a Freeman of the Borough, the official Minute specifically mentions his Chairmanship of the Barking and District Archaeological Society and that he was "particularly interested in the old history of Barking". Moreover the frame of his Citation was "made out of timber taken from the Old Leet House, Barking, AD 1557-1923". Although he had only become a member of the B. & D.A.S. after the War, the carefully prepared and illustrated talk which he delivered at the AGM of 1959, 'Reminiscences of Barking', shows his interest in the history of the town was genuine enough.

"INTERESTING TRAVEL TALKS"

Unfortunately the revived B. & D.A.S. no longer enjoyed the same degree of official encouragement as before the War. Indeed the Society was diminished in other ways. There were now few 'official' members and the impressive list of Vice-Presidents had vanished. Their old President, Robert Muirhead Hewett, died in July 1952 and

Colonel Loftus was voted into the position. The honour seemed well-deserved, but Loftus had retired from Barking Abbey School in 1949 and in 1953 left for Rhodesia to begin his new career as an African education officer. It was not possible to continue indefinitely as an absentee President and eventually he resigned to become a Vice-President. Kenneth Glenny accepted the Presidency in 1958 and proved active in the role despite the pressures of business and of his position as an Alderman of the County of Essex.

C/Ald. Kenneth GLENNY, O.B.E., J.P.
President
1958-1977.

That year also the Programme Card used the unofficial title 'Barking Historical Society' and the new name was officially adopted (unanimously) at the AGM on 11 January, 1960. There were obvious practical reasons for the change - one potential new member had recently been taken aback when told by Mr Fairchild that the Barking Archaeological Society had never conducted a 'dig'. In retrospect, however, one wonders if the change of name also indicated some change of emphasis since, unlike many contemporary societies, it did not call itself a Local History Society.

The post-war Society appeared now to be running smoothly with a full complement of lectures and excursions. These last seem to have become the most popular activity - by the late 1950s the indefatigable Cecil Hustwayte was running three a year. The lectures themselves were developing a tendency to ramble much further afield than Becontree Hundred or even Essex. In 1961 Ken Marshall, Curator of the Passmore Edwards Museum, delivered the March lecture on 'Ilford Hospital Chapel - recent excavations'. But in January a Mr Pearmine had talked about 'A Holiday in Italy', in February a member had given a talk on 'Oberammagau', and in April, Ken Neale was booked to speak on 'Malta, island of antiquity'. The Hustwaytes did deliver a talk on Ilford in the autumn, but at the end of the year members were informed that "Mr and Mrs Pearmine will give another of their interesting travel talks" in January 1962. This programme was not quite typical and can be partly blamed upon the difficulty of obtaining speakers, yet the impression left is that the Society was tending to become a general Historical Society with an increasing proportion of 'passive' as against 'active' members. Nor does this seem to have increased membership; there are indications of a fall in the 1960s.

Since there is abundant evidence for increasing activity in the research and publicising of local history during the '50s and '60s in Barking and elsewhere one can only conclude that the Barking Society was no longer acting as a focus for this interest even when its individual members were closely concerned.

In contrast to Fairchild at Barking, O'Leary was assiduously extending his local collection at Valence, buying not only books but photostats of important documents relating to Barking as well as Dagenham in the Public Record Office and the rapidly expanding Essex Record Office. He personally went hunting for relevant material in other collections. For example, in 1950 he rediscovered the manuscript of Lethieullier's 'History of Barking' in the Hulse collection at Breamore House where according to an oft repeated tale it had been destroyed by fire in 1857.

John Gerard O'LEARY, (Dagenham Librarian 1929-1965). Chairman c.1948-52. Vice-President 1953-1985.

In 1951 he took on the Secretaryship of the Essex Committee of the revived Victoria County History. The first Treasurer to the Essex Committee was Mr Claude Chown. After much effort - not the least of which was in obtaining financial contributions from Local Authorities - the first volumes appeared. These included Vol.5 in 1966, essential reading for anyone interested in the history of Barking, Ilford and Dagenham.

In 1954 another work of great interest to Barking was published which had been in preparation for some years. This was the History of Barking Abbey of which Loftus and H. F. Chettle were joint authors. Also, in 1961, Sister Winifred Sturman of the Ursuline High School at Ilford produced a London Ph.D. Thesis on 'Barking Abbey' and O'Leary bought a copy for the Valence Library where she had done much of her research.

Stephen Jewers, whilst Town Clerk, had drawn the attention of Oxley to the beautifully bound volumes of Vestry Minutes in the Town Hall strong-room from which he had drawn extracts for his Century of Progress. Dr Oxley, having used them for his own History of Barking, realised their great potential and the Barking Borough Council courageously agreed to fund a full study. The volumes were temporarily transferred to Southgate Town Hall, near where he was now living, and in 1955 Barking Vestry Minutes and Other Parish Documents was published: a 344 page study of local government during the 18th and 19th centuries of more than local importance. After this Dr Oxley was the obvious choice to write the sections on 'Barking and Ilford', 'Barking', and 'Ilford' for the V.C.H.,Essex, Vol.5.

Nevertheless Dr Oxley, still faithful to his position as Editor of Publications to the B. & D.A.S., continued to send reports to the AGMs of the Society and to prepare material for Transactions. He had realised that their resources would not be adequate to publishing his Barking Vestry Minutes, but he transcribed 'The Account Book of the Cellaress of Barking Abbey' which they published by duplicating on 19 sheets of foolscap in 1957. Two years later, in 1959, it was 'The Account Book of the Office of Pensions' duplicated on 12 sheets. 'The Early Records of the Barking Monthly Meeting of the Society of Friends' - 10 sheets thought to be researched by H. H. Dawson - followed in 1961; and finally around 1962 'The Accounts for the Destruction of Barking Abbey 1540-41'. Copies of Transactions were distributed to each paid-up member.

Unfortunately these copies - particularly of the last two Transactions - rarely survive because they were neither printed nor bound. Why were they not printed like those in the '30s? The main reason was undoubtedly the great increase that had taken place in the cost of printing. Why then was better quality duplication in book format and binding with a stiff cover not employed instead? This was suggested by John O'Leary who had successfully employed such methods for Valence Museum publications. It would seem that this must also have been rejected by the majority on the grounds of cost. In fact the Society expended £10 on the Transactions of 1959.

Surprisingly, until 1957 the subscription had remained at the original 5s per annum and in that year it was raised, but only to 7s 6d. And although the Library charged them less than 30s p.a. for accommodation, they were carrying forward balances of only around £25 - sometimes substantially less - each year. They had no reserves, and there does not appear to have been any attempt to build up a publications fund or even to solicit donations for occasional publications submitted by their talented Editor.

Ultimately therefore the problem would seem to have been one of policy. It is curious to reflect how different that policy might have been if Dr Oxley had been living nearer and able to attend meetings - as it was, Westminster College moved to the Oxford area in 1959 taking him yet further from Barking; or if John O'Leary had been the Librarian of Barking and Secretary of the Society. Or were members now too absorbed in "interesting travel talks" and excursions to be concerned overmuch with local history in their own area? A congregation which has lost its faith is not likely to spend much on evangelism.

But perhaps the 'founding fathers' were too parochial and indeed somewhat unrealistic when they defined the Objects of the Society back in 1934? In any History Society those who actually study the materials of history in their locality and actively engage in research into documents or the recovery of artefacts are going to be in a minority. Yet, in retrospect, a suspicion lingers that the Barking Society at this time should have been more in touch with contemporary exploration and discovery in the Barking area and keener to support research.

The present writer must declare at this stage how much his growing interest in local history was fostered by the enthusiasm of John O'Leary, by the exhibitions which he held at Valence to interest and educate the public, and by the materials he had assembled to absorb the student once attracted into his library. Equally, writings such as Oxley's <u>Barking Vestry Minutes</u> showed what interesting lands had remained unexplored. Then 'what transports of delight' seized the writer when Providence revealed a cache of 500 Barking parish documents which had eluded Oxley and provided a route into more new territory. Also instrumental in this discovery was former Churchwarden, Mr Harold Wand, who was to become a personal friend and ultimately President of the Barking Historical Society. But I felt no urge at the time to join the Historical Society; I was not sure how much we had in common.

DIVERSITY

1965 and adjacent years saw a number of changes affecting the Historical Society indirectly and directly. Under the London Government Act (1963) the two Boroughs of Barking and Dagenham were united into a single London Borough from 1 April 1965. Their Library Services were merged under W. C. Fairchild, and John O'Leary retired since he was the older man. As a result of his added work-load Fairchild now resigned from the post of Secretary of the Society which he had held for so long. His place was taken by Miss

Norah Dane, daughter of Alderman F. H. Dane, first Mayor of Ilford. She had been a member since 1953/4 and proved a most methodical and efficient Secretary. Rather appropriately another Ilford teacher, Miss Dorothy Hobbs, founder member of the B. & D.A.S. in 1934, addressed the Society in October 1965 on 'Old Ilford'.

Miss Norah DANE. Chairman 1965-1980. Vice-President.

Miss Dane was to hold office until 1980 but she had to face a number of problems during the first ten years. In 1967, Mrs Hustwayte, who had acted as Treasurer since Mr Lloyd's disablement, died. Cecil Hustwayte tried to carry on both as Treasurer and Programme Secretary, but almost exactly a year later he too died suddenly. The excursions he so ably organised have remained as a tradition in the society. Mr Paul Tully undertook the Treasurer's task but Miss Dane as general Secretary also took programme planning on board.

On 4 April 1967, the Central Library in Ripple Road where the Historical Society had met conveniently and economically since the War was burnt to the ground. Abbey Hall, Axe Street, eventually provided temporary accommodation but it was not until the Central Library reopened in new premises in 1974 that the Society again obtained a comfortable home in its fine new Lecture Hall where we still meet.

In the meantime, in 1971 their now elderly Chairman, Ernest Gowers died; he had occupied the Chair for nearly twenty years. The Society chose another lady from Ilford to fill this post also; the first woman Chairman, Miss Madge Carter, did so with grace and dignity. She remained in office till 1977 and as a Vice-President still attends most meetings even though we celebrated her 80th birthday several years ago!

Miss Madge CARTER. Chairman 1971-77. Vice-President. Celebrating her 80th birthday 1986.

A diversity of interests in history and archaeology was a characteristic which all these new officers shared with their President. Both he and Miss Dane had become founder members of the Friends of Historic Essex in 1954, Ken Glenny also served on the Committee of the Friends. Miss Dane like many teachers was also in the Historical Association. Miss Carter was also a member of the

Friends, but like Mr Paul Tully, was actively interested in archaeology; she gave a talk to the Society on 'Digging' in 1967 and later served as Chairman of the West Essex Archaeological Group and as a member of the Council of the Royal Archaeological Institute (1978-1982).

There was moreover a corporate widening of contacts. In March 1964 the Barking Historical Society was represented at the well-attended meeting in Chigwell, hosted by John O'Leary, which created the Essex Archaeological and Historical Congress. Membership of this organisation brought about more co-operation with other societies and museums and an increased awareness of what was going on elsewhere in the county. It also made it easier to find subjects and speakers for the annual programme - something which had been giving Cecil Hustwayte an annual headache. Eventually, when Mrs Dorothy Lockwood became its Hon. Secretary, Congress began to publish a printed List of Speakers for the benefit of its constituent societies (a second edition is now in preparation).

Around 1968 a more loosely organised regional group of societies was also formed in 'metropolitan Essex' calling itself the Forest Group, and the secretaries of member societies began to swap programme cards and notices of meetings. A separate Ilford and District Historical Society had come into being in 1968 with linkages to Redbridge Libraries. Fortunately the rivalry has always been friendly and the two societies continue to have many members in common - like the present writer who has the honour to be both President of the Ilford Society and a Vice-President of Barking.

At the Barking AGM in January 1964 it had been queried 'as to whether full reports were taken of the talks' and 'Miss Carter offered to take them in shorthand, provided a lamp were available when the talks were given with slides'. This she did and typed up these full reports for duplication until she became Chairman in 1971. Nobody felt quite capable of following such an act. But several members tried their hands at producing notes of the lectures, from which grew a regular newsletter for the Society, eventually enhanced with a pictorial cover and photocopied with the assistance of the Barking Arts Council. By this time the newsletters were being produced by Mr and Mrs Shields; and at this point one can no longer forbear to talk about this remarkable husband and wife team so recently deceased.

Mr and Mrs Shields, or 'Ted' and 'Gwen' to use the names that most of us knew them by, joined the Society in the 1950s. Ted worked in the Civil Service and Gwen in the Barking Library. By the '60s they began to give slide lectures to the Society about their holidays abroad, modelling themselves perhaps on Mr and Mrs Pearmine. These at first concerned East European countries and Ireland, for the Shields never concealed their Marxist sympathies. But soon they were also lecturing on architecture which was Ted's special interest. By the 1980s they had developed a quite astonishing repertoire of illustrated talks on a wide variety of topics - their 1989 list included 62! Sometimes they delivered several lectures a week to different organisations, charging little more than basic expenses. And their readiness to take the place of a missing speaker at very short notice was a godsend to any Historical Society. Gwen was Vice-Chairman of the Barking Historical Society for some years before she took over the Chair from Miss Madge Carter in 1978 - an office which she held until 1983.

Both of the Shields were well-read (they had an exceptionally large library in their Goodmayes home) and, unfettered by family commitments, they attended residential courses on a variety of subjects after they had both retired. Ted had perhaps the wider knowledge but Gwen had a shrewd and well-ordered mind as befitted a professional indexer and an expert Scrabble player. Gwen usually did the talking whilst Ted operated the projector (and woe betide him if anything went wrong!) Their strong political views were seldom permitted to intrude: for a professed atheist Gwen had a remarkable interest in church interiors! In passing, one might remark on the wide spectrum of political, cultural and social differences which the Barking Society has amicably accommodated - Cecil Hustwayte was a zealous Anglo-Catholic who died whilst visiting Thaxted for the Easter celebrations.

BACK TO THE SOURCE

By the 1980s the Shields were finding an increasing interest in local topics. The year following her retirement from the Library in 1981, Gwen took a W.E.A. Course for which she wrote a study on 'The Growth and Development of Barking'. She also researched in some depth the identity of St Ethelburga and the Dissolution of Barking Abbey. None of this work was published, although she did give a short lecture on the occupational structure of Barking in 1851, based on detailed work which she was doing at the time of her death in 1992.

By 1982 Ted had been given the title of Liaison Officer since he was the Barking delegate on a number of organisations such as the Essex Congress and the Committee of the Victoria County History of Essex. He thus became an enthusiastic member of the 'Building and Sites Committee' of Congress under the chairmanship of Mr Ian Robertson, the Curator of the Passmore Edwards Museum. This and his informed interest in architecture and building stood him in good stead in the field of conservation. Ted was able to build up a useful relationship with the Planning Section of the Borough of Barking and Dagenham and to obtain copies of planning applications for alterations to Listed Buildings. And by reporting back to meetings of the Barking Historical Society, and through the medium of the newsletter and personal contacts, he was able to stimulate the interest of members in the subject. Since his death this initiative has been continued by others such as the present Chairman, Mr Fred Ettritch, and by the present writer who represented the Society at the recent Unitary Development Plan Enquiry.

At this point it is revealing to hark back to the changes initiated in the mid-'60s. At his departure the great John Gerard O'Leary left a legacy to the new London Borough of Barking (the 'and Dagenham' was a later inclusion through local demand) which included not only a fine local collection and a museum, but also a staff and a tradition. His historic mantle fell particularly upon James Howson who eventually became Curator-Archivist at Valence; the shoulders were frailer though the spirit was willing.

A regular series of historical exhibitions had become part of the tradition at Valence. 1966 being the 1300th Anniversary of the Foundation of Barking Abbey it was decided to hold another Exhibition. Sponsored by Barking Libraries, Barking Arts Council and the P.C.C. of St Margaret's, it was organised by Jim Howson but held at Barking Central Library (not yet the victim of arson). The present writer assisted Jim with the choice of exhibits and the catalogue entries, and Mr Frank Tingey supervised design and layout on behalf of the Arts Council. But the significant fact relevant to this present history is that there was no input from the Barking Historical Society - even though all three of us were ultimately to become members, and two to become Vice-Presidents.

Another tradition inherited from O'Leary was the <u>Dagenham Digest</u>; from 1948 there were four issues a year with a considerable local history content, published by the Dagenham Libraries. This was continued from 1965 as the <u>Barking Record</u> which passed through 25 issues before it was unfortunately discontinued in 1976. The many excellent articles on Barking and Dagenham history were mostly written by Jim Howson himself. Two on local transport history were contributed by the Ilford expert, Len Thomson (who addressed the Barking Historical Society on various occasions). A few were by other members of Library staff including one in 1966 on 'Barking and the General Strike' by Gwen Shields. With this exception, the input from

Barking Historical Society was minimal until the very last issue of May 1976 where 'The Forgotten Benefactor' by Kenneth Glenny appeared. This was a brilliant little piece of original research which he had already presented to the Society in a Presidential address in 1974, but which was well worth preservation in print.

Vice-Presidents Mr James HOWSON (Barking Curator/Archivist) and Dr James OXLEY, at Cumnor, near Oxford, 1984.

There is little doubt that our erstwhile President, Kenneth Glenny played a significant part in steering the Society back to greater involvement in local research by his own example. Back in October 1963 he gave a talk to the Society on 'Barking in the 1800s' but the text has not survived because it was before Miss Madge Carter began reports of lectures. However a talk on 'Barking Manors' delivered in 1971 showed a more than competent knowledge of sources and their whereabouts. Then in 1974 he initiated the practice of delivering a Presidential address to each AGM, using the title mentioned above, 'A Forgotten Barking Benefactor'. Here he built up a skilful case from various primary sources to show that the St Lawrence Spitel established by the Abbey in East Street during the Middle Ages could be identified with the later Wilde's Almshouses opposite The Bull.

His address at the 1975 AGM with the neatly appropriate title of 'Some Gems From the Parish Jewel Box' demonstrated that he was now working on Parish Registers. One 'gem' tickled this writer so much that he found himself confirming years later that Ann Allbritten really did have a son and daughter baptised 'Barking' and 'Ilford' on 18 March 1770 (sad to say they both died in infancy). And if anybody thought Ken could not complete the hat-trick then they were confounded by his 'Dawsonia - the End of an Era' at the AGM of 1976: a history, based primarily upon personal knowledge, of the Dawson family of Barking architects.

Ken Glenny's own family history was even more closely linked with Barking's history - studying one he was bound to study the other. In October 1976 he demonstrated how thoroughly he had researched his own family tree at a meeting of the Ilford and District Historical Society. The writer was delighted to have been able to tape this - especially since Ken died suddenly in April of the following year without being able to deliver another of his great Presidential addresses to Barking.

Surprisingly, Harold Wand who succeeded him was the first President not to have been a founder member; but the history of the Wand family had also been bound up with that of Barking for almost two centuries. Following in the steps of his predecessor he delivered a Presidential address at the 1978 AGM on the history of the 'Barking Church of England School' of which he was a governor and 'Correspondent'. And even though he moved out to beyond Saffron Walden, Harold drove down the M11 to attend most meetings of the Society of which he was proud to be President. This sense of duty, combined with dignity and courtesy, made him an excellent person to lead the Barking Historical Society into their Golden Jubilee celebrations in 1984.

A cynic might describe a 'Members' Evening ' as the last refuge of a desperate Programme Secretary. But the Society has held some successful sessions in recent decades which fulfilled one object, that of uncovering fresh talent. In January 1976 a new member, Mr Rob Gehringer, impressed members with a selection of his own striking slides ranging from Barking Town Quay through Tilbury Fort to Cornish tin mines and a commentary which revealed a wide range of interests and insights. Upon closer acquaintance Rob turned out to be also an expert collector of 'ephemera' such as pot-lids, jars, bottles, advertising material and similar artefacts - with a zest for excavating Victorian rubbish dumps and investigating the social history of our consumer society.

Harold WAND. President 1977-1991. Beside the 1872 foundation stone of the National School 1982.

Such a fresh approach was most welcome and at the next AGM, when Gwen Shields succeeded Miss Madge Carter in the Chair, the genial Mr Rob Gehringer was elected Vice-Chairman. The writer remembers with much pleasure working with him on several projects - photographing the illustrations in the Frogley MS (a voluntary task which took almost a week of 1979); preparing a combined lecture to deliver to the Society on 'Coastal Defences' in 1983; and the big job setting up the Jubilee Exhibition in 1984. In all these tasks his good-humour and resourcefulness made him a splendid working partner. He took over as Chairman with youth on his side as the Society prepared to celebrate its Golden Jubilee in 1984. At the same meeting the Barking Historical Society resolved to re-introduce 'and District' into their title.

GOLDEN JUBILEE

In 1984, in celebration of their half-century and in tribute to their founders, the Barking and District Historical Society set about assembling the most complete Exhibition of the original Materials of Barking History ever seen in one place at one time. The Barking and Dagenham Library Service gave full co-operation in this ambitious project. Without their backing we could not have hoped to borrow such valuable and irreplaceable manuscripts as the '1456 Abbey Rental' from the British Library, Smart Lethieullier's 'History of Barking' from Sir W. Westrow-Hulse, Edward Sage's 'History' from the Essex Record Office, and Frogley's 'History' from the Essex Archaeological Society. As it was we had to seek far and wide for sufficient secure glass cases to display them.

B. & D.H.S. Golden Jubilee Exhibition 1984 at Central Library, with Gwen and Ted SHIELDS in attendance.

The Society had acquired experience since 1977 in mounting pictorial displays on historical themes at Dagenham Town Shows. But nothing on the scale of this Jubilee Exhibition had been set up since the Barking Abbey Exhibition of 1966 in which, as we have seen, the Society took no part. We were therefore very glad to have the advice and assistance of our old friend Jim Howson from Valence with whom the writer and latterly Rob Gehringer were used to working. Jim Howson and the writer helped each other, much as in 1966, with the selection of exhibits and the preparation of the Catalogue; the ever youthful Miss Madge Carter did the typing. Rob showed a flair for display work in the captions and lay-out of the six, colour-coded, sections of the exhibition, whilst other members provided skilled (and unskilled) labour. Gwen (recovering from an operation) and Ted Shields gave many hours to sitting at the desk between the 5th and 10th of November guarding the exhibits and selling catalogues.

The Catalogue, <u>Sources of Local History</u>, is still a useful guide to any researcher, although now out of print. The concluding paragraph of the Introduction is worth repeating, "This Exhibition ... aims to show forth the contribution not only of the past and present members of the Barking and District Society, but also the work of earlier local and county historians upon which they drew. It includes therefore not only printed books like Morant and Lysons, or Shawcross and Tasker, which can be seen in many libraries, but also important manuscript histories which were never printed like those of Lethieullier, Sage and Frogley, which can usually only be seen in photostat. Examples are also shown of the types of primary sources - manuscripts, maps and illustrations - upon which all histories are ultimately based. Some exhibits, like the Frogley MS and Court Rolls of the Manor of Barking, have only become accessible within the last few years and so much of the material they contain still awaits use by future historians. The process of 'exploring the records' is an endless adventure".

Guests at the Golden Jubilee Reception on the 7th of November 1984 at Barking Central Library included the Mayor and Mayoress of Barking, the Mayor and Mayoress of Redbridge, the Bishop and the Rector of Barking, the County Archivist (Mr Vic Gray). Representatives of many Essex societies and two founder members (Dr J. E. Oxley and Mr C. H. I. Chown) and their wives were present. A taped message of greetings was sent from the 100 year old Colonel Loftus in Zimbabwe.

James Howson, by now a Vice-President of the Society, retired in 1986. But the Borough Libraries continued to give support, and even give increased support, for local history (we were now beginning to learn that buzz-word, 'heritage'). Miss Susan Curtis, the new Curator at Valence House Museum, addressed the Society for the first time in March 1988. In that same year the Museum began to open daily to the public. In the 1990s the Barking and Dagenham Library Service embarked upon a liberal programme of publication in the local history field. John O'Leary would have rejoiced, but by an ironic coincidence the old 'Chief' after a sad period of incapacity had died the year before James Howson retired.

*Col. Ernest A. LOFTUS.
President
1952-57.
Vice-President
1958-1987.
Died Zimbabwe
1987 aged 103.*

COL. E. A. LOFTUS,
O.B.E., T.D., D.L., M.A., B.Sc.

FORWARD TO THE DIAMOND

A period of steady progress might have been hoped for following the success of the Golden Jubilee Exhibition and attendant publicity. There was indeed a marked increase in membership over the next few years even though the annual subscription had been raised to £3 in 1984. Interest in the history of Barking Abbey was greatly stimulated as a result of excavations carried out between 1985 and 1986 by the Passmore Edwards Museum. This was the most important archaeological work conducted in Barking since Clapham's 'dig' in 1911, and although carried out on a site immediately adjacent to the west produced a wealth of early medieval finds in contrast to Clapham's meagre harvest. Below later structures, were revealed the remains of Saxon buildings, wells and even a water-mill whose timbers could be dated back to the first century of the Abbey's existence. Associated finds of coins, pottery and other artefacts confirmed these datings.

Mr Rob GEHRINGER. Chairman 1984-88. Viewing excavation of Abbey culvert 1985.

Although few members of the Historical Society actually participated, members were kept well informed of the discoveries by lectures and announcements. In the first half of 1986 there were two lectures by archaeologists from the Passmore Edwards Museum: Mike Stone who had been in charge on the Barking site, and Mark Redknap who dealt both with the Barking site and with Little Ilford church where he had been supervisor. In the same year the Society sponsored this writer's Transaction, Where Was the First Barking Abbey, which, examining both documentary evidence and the new archaeological evidence, challenged the thesis of Colonel Loftus that the Saxon foundation had been on a completely different site to the later Abbey.

But clouds were gathering. It is the misfortune of good Secretaries and Treasurers to be soon taken for granted; it is only when they are no longer available and the affairs of a Society are no longer running smoothly that their value is fully appreciated. In 1980, Miss Norah Dane, who had combined the tasks of General and Programme Secretaries ever since 1965, decided, not unreasonably, that it was time to retire. A new member, Miss Thorn, took on the post but withdrew after only two years. An established member, Mrs Jean

Buck, took over from her in 1983 and proved her abilities during the Jubilee celebrations and the years immediately following.

Then the storms began. In 1987 Mrs Jean Buck, finding the burden too great in changing personal circumstances, offered to continue to arrange the programme providing someone else could be found to undertake the other secretarial duties. The posts were duly divided and several volunteers attempted to do the job of general Secretary over the next year or two, with only limited success. Meanwhile that popular Chairman Mr Rob Gehringer, having decided to set up in business on his own, found it impossible to devote enough time to the Society and in 1989 his Vice-Chairman, Mr Fred Ettritch, took over the Chair. Then in 1990 the Treasurer, Mr Paul Tully, found that his business commitments also were making it difficult for him to continue in that office (he resigned in May 1991 having completed no less than 23 years service!). And in that same unfortunate year of 1990 Ted Shields died.

This administrative crisis revealed itself at the AGM at the end of 1990 when neither Secretary nor Treasurer arrived (the Accounts were in fact submitted and approved at the next meeting). Following this fiasco Mrs Dorothy Lockwood, who had recently retired from the position of Secretary of the Essex Congress, offered to act as Secretary of the Barking Society until a new team could be formed to take over from her. This she did successfully and Mrs Terri Runchman took over as Secretary in 1992 with Miss Lilian Watts as Treasurer in succession to Mr Paul Tully. Mrs Lockwood agreed to continue to help out by arranging programmes with Mr Alf Adams.

It is doubtful if the average member had realised that anything much was wrong. Thanks to the advance programme arrangements made by Mrs Jean Buck business appeared to continue as usual. Indeed during 1990 another 'Transaction' (though the term was not used this time) was written by President Harold Wand under the title of <u>A Short History of the Barking Church of England (Aided) Primary School</u>. (A less forbidding title might have been given to this interesting booklet). It is remarkable that this was a year after the Society had celebrated their President's 80th birthday by presenting him with a framed picture of 'The Paddock' in East Street reproduced from the Frogley MS. The production was handled in the main by our new Chairman, Mr Fred Ettritch, and his Vice-Chairman Mr Doug Waters who represents the Society on the Barking Arts Council. Sadly, President Harold Wand, who had given strong support to the Society through all difficulties, passed away in September 1991; the Mayor of Barking and members of the Wand family were amongst the many who attended the memorial lecture given in his honour by the

Society the following year. Mrs Gwen Shields, now a Vice-President, also died early in 1992.

Chairman Fred Ettritch is himself an enthusiastic collector of material relating to the recent past of his beloved Barking and a staunch defender of its older buildings (and his allotment!) against those who prate of 'Progress'. During 1989 he sought illustrative material from Barking and Dagenham firms for a display on 'Barking Industry over the Last 100 Years' at Eastbury and the Town Show. He contributed his own Reminiscences to newsletters in 1989, 1990 and 1994. In 1989 he also contributed an article on 'The terrible Explosion and Fire at a Barking Chemical Works in the Year 1917'. In 1993 he published his study of <u>The History of Gascoigne Road School 1890 to 1931</u> in the form of an extended newsletter. In the opinion of the present writer this was a mistake; it deserved to have been published in a more permanent form.

As may be gathered from the last paragraph, the Society has not only continued to support the Town Show in most years, but has been putting up displays elsewhere in conjunction with the Arts Council and others. For example they mounted a display at the Essex History Fair at Maldon in June 1991. So important has this activity become that the Society decided in 1991 to purchase its own Display Stands. Pictures have been borrowed from various collections, including that of the writer, but the Barking and Dagenham Libraries' collection at Valence House continues to be the most important source.

A major phenomenon of the last twenty years has been the rapid growth of Family History societies. In our area, the Essex Family History Society was launched in 1974 by the late John Rayment. The East of London Family History Society followed in 1978, whose first Chairman was Mr Fred Filby of Ilford (who was also a prime mover in persuading the Mormons to make the International Genealogical Index available in this country). As a result of increased membership and a demand for local venues the East of London now has four branches - the nearest of which, the Barking and Dagenham branch, began monthly meetings at the Central Library in January 1989.

The challenge to local Historical Societies was not just a question of quantity of members, it extended to the nature and quality of activities. Family History societies began publishing material in local history fields which many Historical Societies had ignored. For example, in our area, the East London Society in 1984 published most useful <u>Indexes to the 1851 Census</u> for <u>Barking, Dagenham and Ilford</u>.

By the 1990s the Barking Historical Society could no longer ignore the impact; the alternatives had to be rivalry or cooperation. Fortunately the latter course was followed. The two societies had already exchanged some speakers and shared some members. In March 1992 they held a joint Open Day in the new St Margaret's Centre which was an outstanding success, and more such ventures have been arranged. The number who belong to both societies has increased and includes Mrs Terri Runchman, the present Secretary of the Historical Society. And now members of both are participating in a joint working-party to index the Frogley MS. The writer is delighted, not only because he strongly favours such cooperation but because he urged the value of making such an index upon the Ilford Historical Society in a lecture 25 years ago!

REFLECTIONS

What opinion would the Society's founders have of our situation? Fred Brand would be envious of our opportunities "to explore the historical records" and publish the results. Record Offices have multiplied and the range of records available has expanded enormously. Record Offices have become 'user-friendly' and introductory books and 'aids to reference' make it relatively simple to embark on voyages of discovery. The study of documents is no longer the prerogative of post-graduate students, professional historians and a few intrepid amateurs. Our concept of useful sources has been broadened to include photographs, maps, packaging materials, taped memories of old people and so on. Technology has assisted with cheap photocopies, audio and video taping, micro filming, computer storage, Desktop Publishing, and colour enlargements for displays.

Fred Brand would rejoice to find Record Offices and Libraries, supported by Local Authorities, publishing local history books and pictures and sponsoring exhibitions. He would realise that such developments had been pioneered by men like John O'Leary. He would probably be pleased with affiliated organisations at local, county and national levels holding meetings and running courses. Knowing the width of his interests we hope he would be attracted by the variety in our lecture programmes, and Cecil Hustwayte would approve our excursions. They would surely both see newsletters as a useful innovation.

As always new opportunities present new problems. When the Society achieves its century what will the members of 2034 think about the way we solved ours?

SOURCES AND ACKNOWLEDGEMENTS

In part this book is an amplification of my 'Introduction' to - Barking and District Historical Society, <u>Jubilee Exhibition Catalogue 'Sources of Local History'</u> 1984.

The first three Sections viz. 'Genesis', "A Happy Thought" and 'Prime' are based principally upon the printed Barking and District Archaeological Society, <u>Transactions 1935-1939</u> and reports in the <u>Barking Advertiser</u>, together with publications named in the text. These sources are supplemented by conversations on this period with Mr Claude Chown and Dr James Oxley, whose friendship I was privileged to enjoy. I am also most grateful to Mr Robert Jewers for information regarding his grandfather and to Messrs Clifford and Keith Glenny for assistance in respect of Stephen Jewers and the Gower family.

Less written evidence has survived for the Section 'Survival and Revival' and the beginnings of 'Diversity'. Earlier James Howson discovered a few programme cards and notices of meetings kept by John O'Leary at Valence. Further assistance has been given and papers loaned by Mr Claude Chown, Miss Joan Harrison, Mr Paul Tully, Miss Norah Dane and Miss Madge Carter. In respect of Ernest Gower, I am most grateful to his daughter-in-law Mrs Doris Gower for information and to Ms E. Pryor of the London Borough of Barking and Dagenham for locating his citation.

Ample documentation - programmes, newsletters, etc. - exists for the later Sections. Personal memories link extensively with this material: I joined the Society c.1974 but had earlier associations indicated in the text.

See also my <u>Sources and Development of Local Historical Studies in the Barking and Ilford area</u> (Ilford & District Hist. Soc.) 1973.

My most grateful thanks are due to my son Richard Lockwood, my good friend Bryan Weaver who prepared this work for publication, and also to my wife Dorothy Lockwood for assistance in many directions.

PICTURES: Barking & Dagenham Libraries, Mr C.H.I. Chown, Miss N. Dane, Mr K. Glenny, Mr G.S. Sanders-Hewett.

FOUNDATION
BARKING AND DISTRICT ARCHAEOLOGICAL SOCIETY
OFFICERS AND COMMITTEE 1934-5

President: The Marquess of Salisbury, K.G.

Vice-Presidents:
The Lord Bishop of Durham
The Lord Bishop of Chelmsford
The Lord Bishop of Barking
The Lord Bishop of Barrow
The Lord Bethell
Sir H Westrow Hulse, Bart
Sir Thomas Bethell

Chairman: R.M.Hewett, Esq., J.P.
Vice-Chairman: F.J.Brand, Esq.

Committee:
W.Anderson, Esq.
H.B.Johnson, Esq.
H.H.Dawson, Esq.,L.R.I.B.A.
Col.E.A.Loftus, M.A.,B.Sc.

Hon. Secretary: J.E.Oxley, Esq.,M.A.
Hon. Treasurer: S.A.Jewers, Esq.

DIAMOND JUBILEE
BARKING AND DISTRICT HISTORICAL SOCIETY
OFFICERS AND COMMITTEE 1994

President: G.S.Sanders-Hewett, Esq.

Vice-Presidents:
Miss M.A.Carter
Miss N.C.Dane
N.Gunby, Esq.
C.H.I.Chown, Esq.,F.C.A.
R.Gehringer, Esq.
H.H.Lockwood, Esq., B.A.

Chairman: F.W.Ettritch, Esq.
Vice-Chairman: D.J.Waters, Esq.

Committee:
W.H.George,B.A.
Mrs J.Lines
Miss J.Harrison
Mrs D.Lockwood
Miss J.Wittred

Hon. Secretary: Mrs T.Runchman
Hon. Treasurer: Miss L.Watts